10 WORDS THAT WILL IMPROVE YOUR LIFE

Expanded and Updated Version of
The Butterfly Effect:
10 Words That Transformed My Life

10 Words That Will Improve Your Life

Expanded and Updated Version of The Butterfly Effect: 10 Words That Transformed My Life

Cover and interior design by Joseph Averitt
Printed by TampaPrinter.com

ISBN 978-0-615-82327-0

Unless otherwise indicated, all scripture references are taken from the Holy Bible, King James Version.

The King James Version is public domain in the United States. Scripture quotations marked (NIV) are taken from the Holy Bible,

New International Version ®. NIV®. Copyright © 1973, 1978, 1984, by International Bible Society. Used by permission of Zondervan. All rights reserved.

Scripture quotations marked (NASB) are taken from the New American Standard Bible®, Copyright © 1960, 1962, 1963, 1968, 1971, 1972, 1973, 1975, 1977, 1995 by The Lockman Foundation. Used by permission. (www.Lockman.org)

Scripture quotations marked (AMP) are taken from the Amplified Bible®, Copyright © 1954, 1958, 1962, 1964, 1965, 1987 by The Lockman Foundation. Used by permission. (www.Lockman.org)

Scripture quotations marked "NKJV™" are taken from the New King James Version® Copyright 1982 by Thomas Nelson, Inc. Used by permission. All rights reserved.

Scripture quotations marked (Message) are taken from The Message Bible (registered trademark sign goes here), Copyright (copyright sign) 1993, 1994, 1995, 1996, 2000, 2001, 2002. Used by permission of NavPress Publishing Group.

Scripture quotations marked (NLT) are taken from the Holy Bible, New Living Translation, copyright 1996, 2004. Used by permission of Tyndale House Publishers, Inc., Wheaton, Illinois 60189. All rights reserved.

10 WORDS
THAT WILL IMPROVE YOUR LIFE

faith

purpose

authenticity

principle

discipline

accountability

courage

perseverance

forgiveness

love

Updated & Expanded Edition of "The Butterfly Effect"

FROM BESTSELLING AUTHOR AND PASTOR
PAULA WHITE

TABLE OF CONTENTS

DEDICATION

This book is dedicated to all of my Paula White Ministries Covenant Partners and Friends!

Since the Ministries inception, you have helped our media ministry grow from our initial broadcast with a single camera, a black backdrop and rent-to-own furniture—to touch over 150 nations, and a potential audience of 2.3 billion people with our daily broadcast.

I pray these "10 Words"—will supernaturally transform your life as well…just as you have helped me transform millions of lives, heal millions of hearts, and win millions of souls worldwide. One day we will stand before the Lord and I know He will honor and reward you for your labor of love to every life that has been touched.

When I was saved at 18 years of age, God showed me in a vision that I would reach the nations for His glory and goodness; that every time I opened my mouth masses of people were saved, healed, and delivered through the manifestation of God—and when I shut my mouth they fell into darkness. In that vision God called me to preach the gospel—and out of that vision, I have dedicated my life to being a vessel for His will on this earth.

The mission of Paula White Ministries—to transform lives, heal hearts, and win souls – has touched and impacted countless millions of lives around the world…and it could never have been done without you—my Covenant Partners and ministry friends. So it is with deep love and respect that I dedicate this book, "10 Words That Will Change Your Life," to you. God bless you, I love you—and I pray that these 10 words help transform you according to God's will for your life, as they have mine.

INTRODUCTION

Words are powerful. God spoke, and from nothing, all things were made. From this moment, words have been a creative force in our universe, containing the innate ability to bring change. To tear down and to build up; to launch wars and to save lives; to imprison and to liberate all reside in the efficacy of words. They bring success to some and distress to others, leading one and impeding another. Jesus used words to impart hope, strengthen the week, heal the sick, and raise the dead. God's inspired words can bring life. They can speak to bones and cause them to rise up and become alive with sinew and muscle. Words can and will frame your life. God shares His love, purpose and power with you and me through His illuminating word.

I love the power of God's words to make someone a new creation. His words changed me from an abandoned, hurting, lonely, broken girl with no direction, to a vessel of God proclaiming those same words of life to the world. So, it is words that I want to give you in this reflective book.....10 of the most powerful words that transformed my life, and I pray these ten words change yours as well.

Because of the incredible transforming power of these 10 core concepts, I originally called this book "The Butterfly Effect", relating to the theory that one small change in a complex system can have the impact of complete metamorphosis into a new, supernaturally alive and thriving creature in Christ. Instead, I have decided to say it in clear and concise terms, exactly how it is and has been for me. The ten words that most activated the transforming power of God in me. Just as Christ's words have breathed life into my circumstances, let these ten words bring you the sustenance and the power to be victorious in every area of your life. You are called to be more than a survivor. You are called to be a child of promise! His word has healed me, carried me, called me, readied me, kept me and lifted me and it can do the same for you. I want you to savor the incredible destiny and purpose God has for you through His word. Within this book, you will not only be inspired by how God has worked in the lives of others but also learn some practical ways to begin putting God's word to work in your life immediately. By design, the book is divided into 10 principles—chapters that have core words that will bring the needed transformation in your life. I have also included space for you to reflect on and record how God is working in your life. As you apply these principles, which have been gleaned from His word, you will walk in His design to fulfill your unique purpose. I am confident that these 10 words will unlock God's greatness in you, so that you will be conformed to His image and that you will be inspired to become all He has destined and desires for you. Begin your journey today!

chapter one: **faith**

"My faith has been developed by the Word that has been deposited."

F aith. It is a calm confidence in God that will cause mountains to be moved. You cannot write the story of this ministry, or my life for that matter, without it. Faith is where my life really began. God reached down in His love and compassion and rescued a broken, hurting girl. He took me with all my baggage and transformed my life into His "daughter of destiny," to break through barriers and birth His plan and my purpose in the earth. The starting point of my personal transformation was when I came to the knowledge of who God is and how to have a personal relationship with Him through His Son Jesus. It was when I surrendered, accepting Christ as my Savior, and was born again, and my carnal mind that I'd grown so used to serving began a process of change. I began walking in faith, fueled by God's Word.

Faith is the first life-changing word and divine principle of value that God ignited in my heart. From humble beginnings of God teaching me to trust Him for my daily needs to seeing masses of multitudes of lives changed for His glory, faith was the foundation for all manifestation. Armed with nothing but a BIG God and a BIG PROMISE, we launched this daily media ministry on faith 10 years ago to transform lives, heal hearts and save souls.

WHAT THE BUMBLEBEE DOESN'T KNOW

God stirred my heart, always with His vision for souls and reaching lives with the good news of the gospel at the forefront. I knew He was telling me, "Now is the time to launch TV ministry." It hardly made sense! Anyone who worked with me back in those days knows how many times we had to retake me just trying to say "God bless you" in front of a camera. It was not a "pretty picture". I had no natural ability. No confidence. No resource or training to pull from. I had nothing but a word from God that said it would be so. But in faith and obedience I was willing to go for it.

I didn't know you were supposed to have capital of a million dollars or more in the bank when you started a TV ministry or a partner base and the appropriate equipment. We started Paula White Ministries with nothing but a promise from God, one camera, some rent-to-own furniture, one secretary that typed about 23 words per minute, six rotary-dial phones and one computer!

I didn't know that we couldn't do it that way, just like the bumblebee. Did you know the bumblebee cannot fly? Neither does he. The bumblebee's body is too heavy for his wings. According to science, he shouldn't be able to fly. But nobody told the bumblebee. It was like that with our media ministry and virtually all that God has called me to do in the earth.

In the natural, there was no way of launching or surviving in that arena. But God's favor makes a way. And His favor was unleashed in abundance because of our willingness to obey and trust Him in faith. When you honor God first, everything else falls into place!

Today, we reach over 150 countries daily, ministering to a potential

2.3 billion people worldwide. In hind site, I now clearly see that Paula White Ministries exists because of the lessons of faith God had given me as a young Christian. No matter what the size of the assignment it will take faith, for without it you cannot please God (Heb 11:6).

FAITH STEPS

Every major work God has done in my life has started with a step of faith. Without Walls International Church began when my family moved to Tampa with nothing but a desire to serve God. We reached out to the indigent by feeding the hungry, clothing those in need, and sharing the Word in the community. Some of the people we worked with had begun to call us their pastors. Through God's favor, a man gave us use of a small office space on Manhattan Avenue in Tampa. It was very tiny, but it was a start. A handful of faith-filled people wallpapered and painted and we began holding Bible studies and doing outreach. It was a humble beginning that required us to use our faith muscles . . . a lot.

We started our ministry without taking any salary and there were times when all we had was our faith. It wasn't always easy. I remember when my son Brad was 5 or 6 years old, we literally had no food one night. I made a phone call to say the refrigerator was empty and we had nothing to eat. There wasn't even a box of baking soda in that refrigerator.

The person I was talking to starting laughing! I was not in the mood or mindset for that response. Then he said, "I'm about to write a best-selling book and become a millionaire. It will be called, 'We stepped out on faith and we are the first ones God failed.' " I hung up the phone frustrated. Then I decided to pray and do something about it.

I remember saying, "Lord, we are here to serve you and you said if we seek you first, you will provide all our needs." I began to speak God's Word over that refrigerator, along with "calling forth" steaks, meat, vegetables and choice foods! By the time I finished praying, there was a knock at the door. A dear woman we knew was at the door with a big box. She said the Lord told her to bring some things to us . . . it was full of food—steaks, chicken, vegetables, dairy! And that's the way it has always been. We have, time and time again, stepped out on faith… only to stand back and testify that God has never failed us!

There is never a time when you have "arrived" in your walk of faith. Your faith can always grow—it is a constant, living, growing principle. My faith lessons continue to this day. Because of the recession and economic turmoil of our nation, walking in faith is more important than ever. Recently, I got word that if we did not raise almost $100,000 in the next 24 hours, our program would be pulled off television. That day I had been preaching at a conference and was running almost two hours late to catch my flight. My assistant told me some people wanted to meet with me quickly before I left. There on the sidewalk outside of my hotel I saw a precious couple with big smiles on their faces. They handed me an envelope and said, "Pastor, God told us to sow into this ministry. God told us we could find you here." Later, when I looked at the check, it was exactly the amount we needed to make up the $100,000! If I had been on time I would have missed them. God has perfect timing.

When you walk in faith, He will meet your needs and supply what He has assigned for you to accomplish for Him. I'm not saying there won't be tough times. But faith is a calm reliance and belief and trust in God no matter what you face.

UNDERSTANDING FAITH

According to Hebrews 11:6, "But without faith it is impossible to please him: for he that cometh to God must believe that he is, and that he is a rewarder of them that diligently seek him." Now, it is important to understand "please Him." It has nothing to do with getting God to like us or approve of us. He already loves you more than you can imagine. And that love is unconditional.

The Greek word for "please" means to come into alignment or to come into agreement with God. It means "fully agreeable". Without faith you cannot fully agree with God. In other words, without the Word working in your life, it is impossible for you to come into alignment or think like God, see like God, act like God, create like God, and do like God. You cannot separate God from His Word. He makes Himself synonymous or "One" with the Word. John 1:1 says, "In the beginning was the Word, and the Word was with God, and the Word was God" (NIV). So without faith, it's impossible for me to line up or agree with God and His Word.

"So then faith comes by hearing, and hearing by the word of God" (Romans 10:17, NKJV). So, if you have faith, or the activated Word of God, you can see God's promises revealed. All you need is a Word, one revelation, which is the unveiling or extraordinary manifestation of what was hidden. You can take that revelation and work the Word and watch the Word work in and for you.

Faith is the Word and the Word is faith. That is why the Bible says God's people perish for lack of knowledge…lack of knowledge of the Word…lack of having the Word deep in their spirits…lack of acting on that Word. Faith is a positive response to God's Word simply because He said so. When we are not in alignment with God, when our minds are not renewed by His Word, there is lack, loss and even death to areas of our life.

Faith always has to do with aligning and joining together with God in full agreement. Everything God has done is done by faith. Everything that manifests tangibly starts with faith. According to Luke 22: 31-32: And the Lord said, Simon, Simon, behold, Satan hath desired to have you, that he may sift you as wheat: But I have prayed for thee, that thy faith fail not: and when thou art converted, strengthen thy brethren. God knew that we would "fail" but prayed that our FAITH fail us not!

THE WIDOW: HERO OF FAITH

The Bible is packed with the most incredible stories of faith. Abraham, Joseph, Moses, Elijah, David, Paul . . . there are so many. But one of my favorite stories of faith is about a woman with no name. God's Word refers to her as "the widow of Zarephath." God thought so much of this woman's faith that He sent the prophet Elijah to her. Her walk of faith is recorded in 1 Kings 17:8-16 (NIV):

Then the word of the LORD came to him: "Go at once to Zarephath in the region of Sidon and stay there. I have directed a widow there to supply you with food." So he went to Zarephath. When he came to the town gate, a widow was there gathering sticks. He called to her and asked, "Would you bring me a little water in a jar so I may have a drink?" As she was going to get it, he called, "And bring me, please, a piece of bread."

"As surely as the LORD your God lives," she replied, "I don't have any bread—only a handful of flour in a jar and a little olive oil in a jug. I am gathering a few sticks to take home and make a meal for myself and my son, that we may eat it—and die."

"Elijah said to her, 'Don't be afraid. Go home and do as you have said. But first make a small loaf of bread for me from what you have and bring it to me, and then make something for yourself and your son. For this is what the LORD, the God of Israel, says: "The jar of flour will not be used up and the jug of oil will not run dry until the day the LORD sends rain on the land." ' "

"She went away and did as Elijah had told her. So there was food every day for Elijah and for the woman and her family. For the jar of flour was not used up and the jug of oil did not run dry, in keeping with the word of the LORD spoken by Elijah."

This woman put faith into action and it saved her life and the life of her son! Just like the Butterfly Effect, the steps of faith you take today can and will impact your future and those around you.

ACTIVATING FAITH IN YOUR LIFE

Strengthening your faith comes by hearing the Word of God, speaking the Word of God and doing the Word of God in your life. Romans 10:17 tell us, So then faith cometh by hearing, and hearing by the word of God. Faith is based on knowing God's Word and knowing God's character and that only comes by spending time through relationship with Him in prayer, meditation and in God's Word.

For years I played the Word of God non-stop in my home. I played it on video tapes, watched it on TV, listened to praise and worship—24 hours a day. It works! What you surround yourself with, the atmosphere you live in, makes an impact on your spirit. The things you allow into the gates of your eyes and ears can have eternal consequences.

When you submerge yourself in the Word, you feed your spirit and grow your faith. Faith produces revelation. And revelation gives you understanding, purpose and connects you with the Spirit of God, allowing you to discover and live out God's original intention for your life. -Faith comes by HEARING ...Hearing means receiving INSTRUCTION.....INSTRUCTION provides INFORMATION.... INFORMATION produces UNDERSTANDING... UNDERSTANDING produces TRUST.... TRUST is Faith... and Faith in God WILL MOVE MOUNTAINS...When you step out and exercise your faith, God will lead you to the next step, and the next . . . until you reach your divine destiny and purpose.

Remember, a little faith goes a long way. Jesus said in Matthew 17:20-21: "If ye have faith as a grain of mustard seed, ye shall say unto this mountain, Remove hence to yonder place; and it shall remove; and nothing shall be impossible unto you. Howbeit this kind goeth not out but by prayer and fasting." Start walking in faith today. You will be surprised at the results.

Practical steps to "Faith" Read God's Word. Speak God's Word. Make time to pray and meditate on God.

Find ways to trust God in small ways each day.

REFLECTIONS

What is faith to you? What does faith in good times vs. bad times mean?

_____

_____

_____

_____

_____

_____

_____

_____

When in your personal life have you lacked faith?

_____

_____

_____

_____

_____

_____

_____

_____

Where in your personal life do you need to exercise more faith?

_____

_____

_____

_____

_____

_____

_____

_____

How many bible verses on "faith" can you find? Write them down and read them daily.

_____

_____

_____

Write out a sequence of "faith steps" you can apply to your life.

Create a schedule to follow daily to activate faith in your life.

What can you do to help others understand FAITH?

chapter two: **purpose**

"We're not to ask why one died, only why
they were born."

Scottish theologian William Barclay once said, "There are two great days in a person's life—the day we are born and the day we discover why."

God designed you perfectly and specifically for a unique task in His eternal master plan—He has a divine purpose for you and you alone. When you understand your distinctive purpose, it is life changing. Knowing you are part of God's great plan on this earth and beyond gives your life greater meaning and excitement. And when you begin living according to that purpose, you will find a fulfillment and joy like no other. I often say, "the definition of frustration is to settle for less than your destiny."

Proverbs 16:4 says "The LORD hath made all things for himself..." The Message version of the Scripture says it this way—"God made everything with a place and a purpose..."

God has a purpose and a plan. His perfect plan is always at work. And you are a part of that plan. Everyone was created for a bigger corporate picture as part of God's plan and purpose, but also, an individual purpose. All of His Word tells us that He has a distinct purpose for you, a plan for your life... one that is secure and satisfying—that's a life on purpose!

The great news is that He is equipping you, strengthening you and preparing you for your divine destiny and His design. In fact, He is working every day in and through your life to perfect you in the image of Christ so that you can play your role in His eternal purpose on this earth.

WHO, ME?
When I hear the word, "purpose," I am so grateful. God's purpose changed my life. I felt that I was unlovable—a nobody with a truckload of baggage—at least that's what I thought.

My father committed suicide when I was 5 ... I was sexually abused ... and I fought back with eating disorders, over achievement, perfectionism, and a string of meaningless relationships. My life was in shambles, then I met Jesus Christ. Finally, someone who loved and accepted me unconditionally!

He picked up the pieces of my broken life and gave me wholeness, peace, joy, and love. I was somebody in His eyes all along and He had a plan for my life!

Christ gave me unconditional love and a vision for myself and ministry, a glimpse of my purpose, when I was 18 years old:

I saw myself preaching on a mountaintop amid masses of people. As I preached, a mist began to fall on the people, and wherever that mist fell, miracles of salvation, deliverance and healing took place. But when I shut my mouth, they fell off into utter darkness. At the end of the vision, the Lord said to me, "Preach My gospel. Through you I will touch nations, and everywhere you speak I will change lives."

Me? How could God do anything with a broken person like me who had a tainted past? But God was true to His promise. "He who calls you is faithful, who also will do it" (1 Thessalonians 5:24, NKJV).

Just like with me, the life God has put you in is larger than the one you are living, and will always include serving someone besides yourself. Before you can fulfill your ultimate purpose, He prepares you. When I told my pastor I wanted to make a difference, he put a broom in my hand. Then, when I was ready, I moved into the children's church in jeans, T-shirts and whistles. As I continued to walk out my faith, God took me into the inner city of Washington, D.C., reaching out to and loving little broken boys and girls. It was a healing experience for me as well as ministry to them.

I remember putting a dress on one little girl who was about 6 years old. She began twirling around like a princess. You could see how special she felt. And she kept saying, "Look what Jesus gave me! Look what Jesus gave me!" It wasn't what Paula had given her or someone else. Jesus gave it to her. What an amazing feeling to take the love of God in a very tangible way to people who are hurting or going through a difficult season or circumstance.

After the 1992 Los Angeles riots, while ministering in the infamous Watts neighborhood, I had the privilege of seeing over 50,000 people born again. How did I get to LA? I had gone to lunch with a well-known evangelist's wife. I was overflowing with a passion for souls and reaching the lost. As the energy and enthusiasm of God's goodness began to touch her heart, she declared, "I have flown all over the world to pass out Bibles and tell people about the love of God, but I've never done it in my own back yard!" I responded, "Oh, you have flown over the mission field to get to the mission field." She then began to cry and asked if I thought we could do anything in her backyard. She lived in LA and it was right after the riots. Every step of ministry led to the next on my journey to accomplish God's purpose in my life.

Little did I know that when I began sweeping up and cleaning the church, it would eventually lead into worldwide ministry and enable me to testify in front of hundreds of thousands of people around world. God is faithful.

It is never too late to pursue God's purpose in your life. No matter what your current situation, you can become a world-changer!

UNDERSTANDING PURPOSE

What is God's individual intention for your life? What is purpose and how do you discover it? First you must understand who you are in Christ. It's not just what you do … it's much bigger than that!

YOUR LIFE PURPOSE DEFINES YOUR MOST MEANINGFUL DIRECTION IN LIFE—IT IS YOUR MOST SUPREME REASON FOR BEING!

Purpose reflects your principles—what you value most in life. It is your over-arching intention and "who" you are in life. It is you regardless of circumstances. When you identify purpose you can integrate it into everyday life… and make your daily life a living reflection of your purpose. Let me share a few biblical principles about purpose to help you understand the plan God has for your life more clearly.

PURPOSE PRECEDES THE PERSON

God's original intention is His final decision. From the beginning of time, God designed the
world to be a wonderful, fulfilling, and prosperous place for His children in covenant with Him. "In the beginning was the Word, and the Word was with God, and the Word was God. He was with God in the beginning. Through Him all things were made, without Him nothing was made that has been made. In Him was life and that life was the light of men," (John 1:1-4, NIV).

God has always had a purpose and a plan. Isn't it incredible that we were on His mind from the beginning? Jeremiah 1:5 says, "Before I formed thee in the belly I knew thee; and before thou camest forth out of the womb I sanctified thee, and I ordained thee a prophet unto the nations."

God created the purpose before He designed the person. He knew you before you were even born! Psalm 139:13-16 says, "For you created my inmost being; you knit me together in my mother's womb. I praise you because I am fearfully and wonderfully made; your works are wonderful, I know that full well. My frame was not hidden from you when I was made in the secret place. When I was woven together in the depths of the earth, your eyes saw my unformed body. All the days ordained for me were written in your book before one of them came to be."

Imagine . . . God ordered your days and proclaimed your purpose before you took your first breath! There are specific things you were born to do and God has already embedded the gifts and talents you need to accomplish them within you. So, how do you find out what that purpose is?

PURPOSE IS REVEALED THROUGH RELATIONSHIP WITH GOD
Purpose is found and functions in the full purposes of God when you are connected to God. You will never live a life of purpose without a God connection.

When you grow closer to God, you can begin to see His greater purpose and where you fit into the grand plan. Psalm 16:11 says, "You have made known to me the path of life; you will fill me with joy in your presence, with eternal pleasure at your right hand." In order to align yourself individually to the assignment of God, you must comprehend "corporately" what God is doing and how you individually fit in. The key to understanding God's purposes is in the reading of His Word, prayer and fellowship with Him.
And as we read in John 1:1-4, you cannot separate God from His Word. He reveals Himself in and through His Word. Psalm 33:4 tells

us "the word of the Lord is right and true." Psalm 18:30 tells us that "His way is perfect." Therefore, to discover and have success in life we must connect and navigate our lives through the Word of God. Certain insight can only be obtained by the study of Scripture.

The Psalmist writes, "Your Word is a lamp to my feet and a light for my path" (Psalm 119:105). What you know determines how you live. When you know God loves you, desires only the best for you, believes in you, watches over you, and is always mindful of you, that is when you can begin to live with the confidence of someone who knows where he is . . . and where he is going. Psalm 121: 5-8 says, "The LORD watches over you - the LORD is your shade at your right hand; the sun will not harm you by day, nor the moon by night. The LORD will keep you from all harm—he will watch over your life; the LORD will watch over your coming and going both now and forevermore."

When you know "Whose" you are, you can begin to understand the purpose you serve. Ephesians 1:11-12 says, "It's in Christ that we find out who we are and what we are living for. Long before we first heard of Christ and got our hopes up, he had his eye on us, had designs on us for glorious living, part of the overall purpose he is working out in everything and everyone." (The Message)

PURPOSE IS RELEASED THROUGH PASSION
Purpose is connected to passion, the intense emotion, compelling action or strong devotion to something. You have to be led by inspired action fed from your personal passion on your journey to accomplishing God's plan for your life. When you are clear about your passion you ignite purpose.

Your inspiration will lead you to the "how" of fulfilling your purpose all along the way. You may not see the entire journey, but your passion gives you the next step. It is like driving at night on a road only lit by headlights. You cannot see the entire path to your destination, just the lit portion in front of you. This illumination, just a step ahead, will allow you to stay on the road and heading in the right direction until you reach your destination.

To find passion, step out of your busy life and ask yourself :

- What do I love to do?

- What do I care most about?

- What truly matters to me?

- What am I committed to?

- What do I stand for?

- What are my principles?

- What three things do I value the most?

The answers are your passions—they are like a breadcrumb trail leading you to your purpose! Passion is energy of the soul. I believe unique power comes from your passion. So why waste away without passion? The path to fulfillment is making the things that matter most to you a priority in your life.

Make choices every day in favor of what you most care about. That is when your soul will start to sing and lead you to express your self. It will help you express your unique purpose in all areas.

God's Spirit can lead and work through your passion. Romans 8:14 says, For those who are led by the Spirit of God are the children of God. Each day ask God what He would have you to do and where He would have you to go. When led by His spirit you will discover that you are part of something bigger than yourself!

Your purpose is found from your passion. Sometimes that passion-led purpose includes things in life that have caused your pain. It is the places you have bled in life that become your sermon. It is more than learning Scripture, it is living it! Every experience of your journey equips you to relate and be empathetic to others, to understand them. In pure etymology, "understand" means to stand among. It doesn't mean to stand beneath or below. It means to stand with.

The places you have bled are part of what makes you qualified to make a difference in the lives of others. When you realize that what God has done in you is a process that now He wants to do through you, you understand the true meaning of purpose!

NEHEMIAH: LIVING OUT GOD'S PURPOSE

Let's look at the life of Nehemiah in the Old Testament. He went from cupbearer to a great leader, responsible for rebuilding the walls of Jerusalem. And as I was studying his life, I discovered some very specific characteristics and principles in his rise to power that we can learn from.

Just like you, Nehemiah had a purpose, an assignment from God. Nehemiah's story reveals God's position and patterns in calling us to His work. In Nehemiah's story, we can see some important principles for living a life of purpose.

INQUIRE GOD'S PURPOSE.

We see in Nehemiah 1:2 that he first asked questions—"and I asked them concerning the Jews who had escaped, who had survived the captivity, and concerning Jerusalem." You must seek God's intent (Matthew 6:33, Isaiah 55:6). Have you asked God about your purpose and assignment in life? Are you seeking His will? Nehemiah's questions revealed his heart. He asked two things—about God's people and God's place.

PRIORITIZE YOUR ACTIONS.

When Nehemiah heard about the devastation of Israel, what did he do first? He sat down and wept. According to verse 4, Nehemiah dealt with his emotions first and "was fasting and praying before the God of heaven." Get your composure for the task ahead and seek God every step of the way. Develop a plan for your career, for your projects and tasks. Plan and prioritize your actions, starting with prayer and fasting. Give it to God because it's all up to Him and then work like it's all up to you.

BE PASSIONATE.

Nehemiah was passionate about rebuilding the walls. His prayer in chapter 1, verse 11 revealed his passion to succeed. Desire drives passion and passion is the fuel for your power. God doesn't want someone who is "lukewarm" (Rev. 3:15-16)! Without passion you become passive. But passion moves you to your purpose. God designed you with a purpose, a destiny.

Out of compassion and concern for God's people and God's place, Nehemiah receives his mission. Because he cared, Nehemiah moved forward. When you care, you create passion . . . and passion fuels your purpose. Did you move the last time God challenged you with a cause or mission? God never gives you instruction past your last act of disobedience.

He gives you the passion, but you must be the activator. And action must be rooted in and working alongside principle. "Do you see that faith was working together with his works, and by works faith was made perfect?" (James 2:22, NKJV).

EXPECT RESISTANCE.

Once you move forward in your destiny, the enemy gets distressed and angry. When the enemy of God's people, named Sanballat, heard that Nehemiah was moving forward to rebuild the walls, "he was furious and very indignant, and mocked the Jews" (Nehemiah 4:1, NKJV). Immediately, Sanballat asked these questions—"What are these feeble Jews doing? Will they fortify themselves? Will they offer sacrifices? Will they complete it in a day? Will they revive the stones from the heaps of rubbish—stones that are burned?" (Nehemiah 4:2, NKJV).

Satan wants to thwart your divine assignment. In order to do that, he is asking the same questions about you.

Do you know your purpose?

Do you know who fortifies you with the power and ability to accomplish it? Will you sacrifice? Will you give up what's valuable to follow God's purpose? Do you have the determination to finish what God started in you?
Will you raise up the principles and standards torn down and burned by the enemy?

I want to encourage you today to answer these questions for yourself and seek God's purpose for your life. You are a designer's original. And when you truly know who you are and whose you are, you will be an earth shaker and a world changer.

ACTIVATING PURPOSE IN YOUR LIFE

As a child of God, you must realize there is purpose in whatever you do, and however you serve. Everyone is a living epistle. You preach without moving your mouth. Your life shows your passion and purpose every day.

I read a story once about a woman who walked up to a dusty building site where three strong, young men were working hard laying bricks. She walked up to the first man and asked him what he was doing. He replied rather rudely, "Can't you see? I'm laying bricks. This is what I do all day—I just lay bricks." She then asked the second man what he was doing. He replied, "I'm a bricklayer and I'm doing my work. I take pride in my craft, and I'm happy that what I do here feeds my family." As she walked up to the third man, she could see that his eyes were full of joy and his face was as bright as the day. When she posed the same question to him, he replied with great enthusiasm, "Oh, I'm building the most beautiful cathedral in the whole world!"

It isn't what you do in life that defines your feeling of purpose, it is your perspective. Roman 8:28-30 tells us ALL things work together for good to those who love God and who are called to His purpose. That is you! Live each moment inspired by that knowledge.

Consider the passions, talents, and experiences God has placed in your life. Ask Him to lead you to the perfect plan of fulfillment and purpose He has already prepared for you!

REFLECTIONS

Write out a synopsis of what you feel God's purpose is for you.

_____
_____
_____
_____
_____
_____

How has He equipped you for that purpose?

_____
_____
_____
_____
_____
_____

What struggles have you found in your life finding your purpose?

_____
_____
_____
_____
_____
_____

What specific things do you need to fulfill your purpose?

_____
_____
_____

_____

What are some specific things you feel are trying to prevent you from fulfilling your purpose?

_____
_____
_____
_____
_____

Write out a plan to eliminate things hindering your progress.

_____
_____
_____
_____
_____
_____

What does "activating purpose" mean to you?

_____
_____
_____
_____
_____
_____

What can you do to help others understand PURPOSE?

_____
_____
_____
_____
_____
_____
_____

chapter three: **authenticity**

"When you accept yourself, you give yourself one of life's greatest gifts."

One of the most powerful words God used to transform my life was "authenticity." Simply put, authenticity is being true to who God created you to be. Psalm 139:14 says we are "fearfully and wonderfully made." God has given each one of us a unique design— that includes our personality, likes and dislikes, physical appearance, talents, giftings and more. No one has the same makeup. Add to that our very different life experiences that help fashion who we are. There is absolutely no one like you . . . and you will never discover God's unique purpose for your life if you keep trying to live up to other people's expectations and definitions.

Authentic comes from two words. One is "auto," which means self and the other is "hentes," which means being. Authentic means being yourself.

When you live authentically, you find the value of your own voice. In fact, there is great freedom that comes with transparency. You better be yourself—because sooner or later the real you will show up. I learned early on to be true to who God created me to be.

A HEAPING, HELPING OF TRUTH

When I was a co-pastor in my early 20s, I had very little experience in public speaking. We were still struggling to get Without Walls church started when a television broadcast called me to be a guest cook on their show.

I called my mom, got the recipe for her Southern chicken and broccoli casserole, and off I went! Things were going well, I thought, as we prepared the casserole live on air. Suddenly, in the midst of chopping and mixing, the hostess turned to me and said, "So, you were sexually and physically abused...and your father died."

I was caught completely off guard. I didn't think anyone knew. I had never been public with my testimony other than sharing it with the ladies' Bible study. For a brief moment, I froze inside . . . I felt mortified. Then, like a river, my story gushed out of me. I told it all!

Right there in front of the cameras, my life became an open book. I told of the tragic night my father took his life and how, from the time I was age 6 to 13, I was sexually and physically abused numerous times in horrific ways. I shared despite it all, God loved me and changed my life with salvation and an intimate walk of real peace with Him.

When I left the stage my emotions plummeted—I felt depressed, rejected, embarrassed. At that time, people just didn't "reveal their warts" that way! We kept unpleasant things quiet, hidden. With such a painful past, I thought no one would like me or want me around.

But the next day, a lady with tears in her eyes came up to me and said, "Paula I saw you yesterday. Thank you. You changed my life." She began to tell me how broken, hurt, despondent and suicidal she had been. But when she heard me share my story it transformed her. She said she realized that if I could tell what I had gone through, then she could make it through her own trial. That one woman sparked a transparency in my ministry. She helped me understand that we have all been through something to share. But if we can be authentic, transparent and real about what God is doing and has done in us, we can help others. That was really the catalyst that allowed me to openly share my testimony with others and begin living authentically.

LIVING AUTHENTICALLY

Authentic living comes with spiritual maturity. At some point in your spiritual walk, you must realize that God made you perfectly in His sight and that every experience you go through is preparing you for His purposes. I am not saying everything is sent by God, but it is used by Him. Here are some practical steps you can take to begin living authentically.

Deal with the thorns. In the Luke 8 parable about sowing the Word of God, thorns were seed killers. "The seed that fell among thorns stands for those who hear, but as they go on their way they are choked by life's worries, riches and pleasures, and they do not mature" (Luke 8:14). Do not allow worries about your future or about what others think prevent you from trusting God and living true to who He created you to be.

Believe you're all that! No matter where you came from, what you went through, what you did, how many times you fell down, or where you are today, you are incredible in God's eyes. Remember that you are:

- fearfully and wonderfully made (Psalm 139:14.

- God's workmanship (Ephesians 2:10).

- victorious (Revelation 21:7).

- called by God (2 Timothy 1:9).

- more than a conqueror (Romans 8:37).

- ambassador for Christ (2 Corinthians 5:20).

- heir with God (Romans 8:16-17).

- complete in Christ (Colossians 2:10).

- beloved of God (1 Thessalonians).

- chosen by God (Ephesians 1:4).

- reconciled to God (Romans 5:10).

- justified (Romans 5:1).

- sealed by the Holy Spirit (Ephesians 1:13).

- overtaken with blessings (Deuteronomy 28:1).

- seen by God as holy, blameless, above

- reproach (Colossians 1:21-22).

- firmly rooted, built up and strong in faith (Colossians 2:7).

- enabled to do all things (Philippians 4:13).

- always triumphant (2 Corinthians 2:14).

You can be authentic because Christ has equipped you, God loves you and the Holy Spirit leads you.

Trust in God's timing. God is never late. He is never early. He is always right on time. Do not try to rush His plan for your life. "There is an appointed time for everything. And there is a time for every event under heaven" (Ecclesiastes 3:1, NASB). When you try to force God's purposes to fit into the mold you want for your life, you cannot live authentically . . . and you are setting the stage for disaster. Don't force what doesn't fit.

Forget the past. Now, I'm not saying you should hide or cover up your past. But God does want you to move beyond it. The trials and challenges of your life helped get you to where you are today but your journey is not done. Press on! Move forward! Don't allow your past to hold you back. "Not that I have already obtained all this, or have already been made perfect, but I press on to take hold of that for which Christ Jesus took hold of for me. Brothers, I do not consider myself yet to have taken hold of it. But one thing I do: Forgetting what is behind and straining toward that is ahead, I press on toward the goal to win the prize for which God has called me heavenward in Christ Jesus" (Philippians 3:12-14). The voice of your past will only disqualify you from your purpose. But the call of your future will invigorate you to press towards it.

JESUS' WOUNDS: SEEING IS BELIEVING

We can be ourselves . . . because that is exactly what Jesus did. From the time He stayed behind in the temple as a child until He ascended into heaven, Jesus knew exactly who He was and stayed true to that purpose. And one of the great, practical lessons we can learn from Jesus was that He never hid his wounds.

In fact, Jesus knew the power of revealing His own pain and scars to impact the lives of others. I love the story of Doubting Thomas in John 20. Jesus had been crucified, risen from the grave and appeared to His disciples. Thomas wasn't with the others when Jesus came to them at first and was having trouble believing that Jesus had risen from the grave.

"Now Thomas (also known as Didymus), one of the Twelve, was not with the disciples when Jesus came. So the other disciples told him, 'We have seen the Lord!' But he said to them, 'Unless I see the nail marks in his hands and put my finger where the nails were, and put my hand into his side, I will not believe.' A week later his disciples were in the house again, and Thomas was with them. Though the doors were locked, Jesus came and stood among them and said, 'Peace be with you!' Then he said to Thomas, 'Put your finger here; see my hands. Reach out your hand and put it into my side. Stop doubting and believe.' Thomas said to him, 'My Lord and my God!'" (John 20:24-28, NIV).

Jesus knew Thomas needed to see His scars to believe. Jesus, in all of His risen glory, approached Thomas with vulnerability and revealed His wounds. It was as if He was saying, "Look what I've gone through." When we unveil ourselves—when we say, "No more mask"—we are ready to help others understand that they are not alone. When we live with authenticity and transparency, we can face the world as our true selves sharing what God has done in our life!

NO MORE MASK

Do you live behind a mask? Many people live behind masks of perfectionism, passivity, or some other character to conceal their fears, disappointments, feelings of rejection, and vulnerability.

These people never feel "safe," so they create false solutions to cover themselves. But God never intended for you to live behind an emotional masks. Throughout His ministry, Jesus repeatedly denounced the hypocrisy of the scribes and Pharisees, who paraded the appearance of being godly, wearing masks of prayer and fasting (Matthew 6:1–16; 23).

God never intended for us to wear emotional masks, smiling on the outside, but feeling miserable on the inside. God loves us too much for that. He has an authentic, unique and divine life and destiny for each of us. I discovered long ago that as long as I wear a mask, then I am playing the role of a character. And God is not interested in my role-playing or in yours. He wants to deal with you, the real you. He wants to know the you who struggles with secret issues of the heart, the you behind the fake smile and pretty clothes.

Let me challenge you to come from behind your mask. Begin living in truth. If you have asked Jesus to come into your life and forgive you of your sins, there is no need to feel shame for the past. Ask God to give you the strength and courage to live authentically.

Part of living authentically is also accepting others. I believe very much in the power of acceptance—and that God unconditionally accepts us. You cannot change people in your own power, just accept them and pray for them. Make an effort to love others through Christ just as they are and leave it up to God to transform their lives. When you can live authentically, you become a beacon of light and hope to others . . . and you are free to pursue God's perfect plan for your life.
Practical steps to "authenticity" Share your personal testimony with someone. Begin journaling your spiritual walk.
Try to see yourself and others through God's eyes.

REFLECTIONS
Describe your true self.

_____
_____
_____
_____
_____

Write out some life experiences that have molded you into who you are.

_____
_____
_____
_____
_____

Are there others in your life who hide behind false identities? If so, what do you think motivates their behavior?

_____
_____
_____
_____
_____

Are there any lingering spiritual, psychological, or relational hindrances that are holding you back from knowing your "authentic self"?

_____
_____
_____
_____
_____
_____

Write a plan that helps develop the God-given traits that are truly yours and a plan to eliminate any "masks" you maybe hiding behind. Set realistic goals for yourself.

_____
_____
_____
_____
_____
_____

How can you "deal with the thorns," or the seed killers, from now on?

_____
_____
_____
_____
_____
_____

What can you do to help others understand AUTHENTICITY?

_____
_____
_____
_____
_____
_____

chapter four: **principle**

"God's patterns are permanent. His principles are working for you or against you every day. It is the law of God!"

Before you can experience the promises of God, you must first understand His principles. A principle is a fundamental truth or law upon which others are based. It is a rule of conduct. The life- altering word, principle, comes from the root word prince, which means monarch or having to do with dominion. God laid down His specific principles for us throughout His Word to rule over our daily lives.

The abundant life God wants to give you is wrapped up in principles of faith and obedience that are found in His Word. You see, God's Word is always working for you or against you. God established His principles from the beginning. And I believe it is not possible to violate the principles of God and see the promises of God. They are inseparable.

Here's the key to a successful life—understand, embrace and follow

God's principles. God's principles never change. They are fundamental to life. So, if you embrace the habits of God, you will be successful. It is pretty simple.

INSATIABLE HUNGER

I am far from a perfect person, but from the moment I heard the gospel for the first time and dedicated my life to God, I had an appetite for Scripture. That Word is what continues to transform the character of Christ in me daily. I knew I had a heavenly Father who loved me and who had a purpose for my life. Now, I certainly didn't know exactly what that purpose was or how I was going to accomplish it, but I knew the answer was found in God's Word. I held up the Bible and declared, "The answers to life are in here—reveal to me who You are, and who I am. Reveal to me 'life answers'." And for two years, with a passionate hunger and insatiable thirst for the Word of God, I studied day and night.

As I sought God's plan for my life, He gave me a greater hunger to really "excavate" the roots of His patterns and principles in order to teach the Body of Christ. I am passionate about seeing people released from bondage and lack to walking an empowered life in the fullness of what God has given—those precious and magnificent promises available through our true knowledge of Him. Knowledge comes from studying the Word. Then comes revelation, and that is what motivates us to move in faith!

Even when you know God's principles, it isn't always easy to follow His commands in obedience. I remember just after getting our little storefront office/church arranged many years ago, I received an unusual request. I was invited to speak about evangelism and outreach by a Greek Orthodox Church in the area. It was a wonderful opportunity, that was very humbling, to consider me to actually "speak." At the time we still weren't taking any income from our small but faithful congregation for ourselves, so we had very little on which to live. When I was given a $200 honorarium for speaking at the Greek Orthodox Church that night, I was ecstatic. In our financial situation, that $200 was like being given $2 million.

One evening that same week, I attended a service at a local church in Tampa to hear a special speaker, be refreshed and receive the Word. At one point during his message, the guest speaker said, "God is speaking to someone here tonight to give it all." I didn't respond. I just put my head down thinking that $200 was our all, and that surely this moment would pass. Then he said it again. It was as if God was standing right in front of me saying, "What are you going to do?"

All is all…whether you are speaking of $200 or $2 million. Letting go of your all, whether it is $200 or $2,000, is still a sacrifice. I gave that sacrificial seed gift of $200 that night, "my all," trusting God to sustain and bless us. I have to admit, even though I had faith and was obedient, I still "felt" the "price" of sacrificing.

The next day, the door opened suddenly at our church. I looked up to see a lady with red hair, standing at about 5'2" tall, approaching. She walked with purpose, and a little bit of an attitude. I wasn't sure what to expect. She walked in and threw down an envelope and said, "God kept me up all night last night. Here…take it." She abruptly turned and walked out the same way she came in. Inside the envelope was a check for $10,000. I could hardly believe it! To be handed that amount of money the day after "giving it all" with that $200 offering was amazing. But it didn't stop there.

About two hours later, while I was still astounded and in deep gratitude to the Lord over that incredible gift from Him…the same lady came back again. With the same attitude with which she delivered the first gift, she handed over another envelope and said, "Here. God said to give it all," and with that, she turned and marched right back out of the door. That envelope contained a check for $5,000! With that $15,000 offering we rented the auditorium of a nearby high school, and began the first services of Without Walls International Church, a ministry reaching many lives for the glory of God.

A DEEPER UNDERSTANDING OF PRINCIPLES

Why are principles so important? Principles keep us aligned with the will of God. Principles are how we maintain our position under God's headship. There are principles in God's Word that rule over every aspect of our lives. If we want to see God's blessings come to pass, we must be in accurate alignment and order, by following God's principles.

The key is to align yourself with the patterns of God. God's principles can be found in His patterns. These principles were established long before man ever had a revelation or a vision of them. They are unchanging. And as I've said before, God's principles propel you into His promises!

A pattern is an order of arrangement or parts . . . a model or a design from which copies can be made. For every pattern, there is a design and for every design there is a designer. It is not your job to design or to develop, but to discover and implement or put a decision and plan of God into effect. Patterns are established from concept, the original intention, thought or notion.

God's original intention is His final decision. That means God doesn't change His mind—His patterns are permanent. What a release from pressure to try and make life happen, or force something to fit! Proverbs 19:21 reminds us that "many are the plans in a man's heart, but it is the Lord's purpose that prevails." Plans are the contrivance of a mentally fabricated plot. What a waste of time, energy and talent when God's ultimate intention will always succeed! All you need to do is "flow" with the determination of God. You have been positioned, or "accurately arranged," to simply walk out the pattern or predetermined plan of your destiny! You do so by implementing His principles. When a divine principle is implemented, a divine result is reaped.
Because God is a God of patterns, when you follow the pattern, you see the manifestation of the promise from being in position. All covenant privileges are released and received by believing and activating the Word of God. That's why you must have the truth of God's Word operating in your life for all things to comply and agree with the determination of God. That is why principle is a life- changing word.

The decisions you make today to follow God's principles and patterns will determine the quality of life you live tomorrow. Therefore make sure you have the thoughts and mind of Christ directing your daily life! By following His principles, you bring your life into the order God has established. Don't wait until life throws you a "curve" ball. Walk out the patterns of God every single day of your life. When you do, you will build a firm foundation that will not be shaken. The "things" are added to you when the foundation is in place to be built upon. Psalm 11:3 (NKJV) reminds us, "If the foundations are destroyed, What can the righteous do?"

ADAM AND EVE: VIOLATION OF PRINCIPLE

God's Word gives us an example right upfront of the damage that can be done when we violate God's principles. The first principle God released into His creation is found in Genesis 1:26-28:

And God said, Let us make man in our image, after our likeness: and let them have dominion over the fish of the sea, and over the fowl of the air, and over the cattle, and over all the earth, and over every creeping thing that creepeth upon the earth. So God created man in his own image, in the image of God created he him; male and female created he them. And God blessed them, and God said unto them, Be fruitful, and multiply, and replenish the earth, and subdue it: and have dominion over the fish of the sea, and over the fowl of the air, and over every living thing that moveth upon the earth.

God gave Adam and Eve dominion over the creatures of the earth. Dominion means to tread down, to rule, to reign, to prevail. Notice specifically God instructed to have dominion over everything that creepeth on the earth. God's first principle to mankind was "to take dominion" and "be fruitful, multiply, replenish."

The second principle came by way of a policy, a policy being any governing principle. "And the LORD God commanded the man, saying, Of every tree of the garden thou mayest freely eat: But of the tree of the knowledge of good and evil, thou shalt not eat of it: for in the day that thou eatest thereof thou shalt surely die" (Genesis 2:16-17).

But Adam and Eve violated BOTH principles; first by not maintaining dominion over the serpent, the creeping thing and also by eating of the Tree in the middle of the Garden, the tree to knowledge of good and evil. The result of this, we are told in Genesis 3:7, that: "the eyes of them both were opened, and they knew that they were naked; and they sewed fig leaves together, and made themselves aprons."

Adam and Eve experienced a feeling of being uncovered because they had violated God's principles and gotten out of position. Later, when God called to Adam and asked, "Where art thou?" God was really asking, "Where are you in relation to my principles I left for you? Are you in position for my blessing? Or are you out of line?

Principles, in other words, keep us close to God, in alignment, in position to be blessed. When we break God's principles, we cannot see His greatest promises come through in our lives!

LIVING ON PRINCIPLE

So how do you live according to God's principles? First you must understand them. Develop a hunger for God's Word. Read it every single day. Study God's commands. Use study guides and book from others for a greater understanding of God's patterns and principles. Many times, it may not be what you are doing wrong that prevents you from reaping God's blessings, but the fact that you are not doing enough of what is right. Hosea 4:6 says, "my people are destroyed from lack of knowledge." When you know better, you live better.

Once you understand a principle of God's Word, put it into action. For example, another powerful principle of God is "Seed Time and Harvest." In order to take possession of God's promise, you must understand His perpetual system of sowing and reaping—His system of seed time and harvest. This is a law that governs the Kingdom of God. It is much broader than simply finances. The Word of God declares in Proverbs 18:24, "A man who has friends must himself be friendly." It is the law of attraction. You will reap what you sow.

Genesis 8:22 says: "While the earth remaineth, seed time and harvest, and cold and heat, and summer and winter, and day and night shall not cease." Ecclesiastes 3:1 tells us, "There is a time for everything, and a season for every activity under heaven."

There is a season to sow . . . and a season to reap the harvest of what you have sown. Whatever you believe God has promised us—a glorious and great future, family and children blessed and in good health, business or chosen career flourishing—whatever our promise is, God is faithful to fulfill it. But to take possession of the promise, we must put our faith and action together. That which we sow, we will also reap. Galatians 6:7 says, "Be not deceived; God is not mocked: for whatsoever a man soweth, that shall he also reap." So make sure you sow good things. The laws of God are always working for you or against you.

Another principle governs what you sow . . . the principle of First Fruits. Yom HaBikkurim, the Jewish festival celebrating the Feast of First Fruits, is one of the most mentioned feasts in the Bible, second only to Passover. First fruits are the first part of the harvest to ripen. It is the part of the harvest that was given to the priest as an offering to the Lord. Each family was to bring a basket of their first fruits and give it to the priest as the Lord's representative (Deuteronomy 26:1-12). Leviticus 23:10-14 gives specific guidelines for a special first fruits sheaf to the Lord at the time of the Passover festival.

God still considers first things to be holy and devoted to Him, but today first fruits has to do with the practice of keeping the main thing—the main thing, and God IS the main thing! First fruits means the first in place, order and rank; the beginning, chief or principle thing. God says first things belong to Him in order to establish redeeming covenant with everything that comes after. In God's pattern, whatever is first establishes the rest. The first is the root, from which the rest is determined. I have seen over and over again how when you put God first, He will take care of the rest.

Seedtime and Harvest and First Fruits are just two of the many principles God has outlined in His Word. I want to challenge you to dive into Scripture and ask God to reveal His principles to you. Understanding the importance of God's principles has truly transformed my life and it can yours, too!
Practical steps to "principle"

As you read God's Word daily, ask yourself what principle relates to the text. Ask God to reveal His never-changing principles and patters. Focus on putting at least one principle into action in your life this week.

REFLECTIONS

Off the top of your head, write out what you think are some principles of God.

_____
_____
_____
_____
_____
_____
_____
_____

Study the Bible daily for the next year. Write down in detail God's principles and patterns that you discover in His Word.

_____
_____
_____
_____
_____
_____
_____

How can these unchanging principles be applied to your life?

_____

_____

_____

_____

_____

_____

_____

_____

What "principles" have you always followed in your life?

_____

_____

_____

_____

_____

_____

_____

What "principles" do you need to apply in your life?

_____

_____

_____

_____

_____

_____

_____

_____

In what ways do you need to be aligned with God more based on His principles?

_____

_____

_____
_____
_____
_____

What can you do to help others understand PRINCIPLES?

_____
_____
_____
_____
_____
_____
_____
_____

chapter five: **discipline**

"The pain of discipline weighs much less than the heavy load of regret."

D o you ever feel like your life is spinning out of control? If you see a stranger in the mirror who is overweight, stressed out at work, estranged from family, or, most importantly, growing farther from God, you may be wondering what happened. You are not alone. We live in a society without boundaries. Habits, desires, spending and other addictions run rampant. That is why I believe the word "discipline" is so important.

Discipline means control gained by enforcing obedience or order. It is training that corrects, molds or perfects the mental faculties or moral character. Its etymology is from the Latin word "disciplina," which means teaching learning and from "discipulus" meaning pupil.

Through discipline, you can regain control of your life in many ways.

Discipline is particularly important to believers. The word "disciple" comes from the word "discipline." And the importance of discipline cannot be overstated.

God's Word tells us about the role of discipline. Deuteronomy 8:5 says "Know then in your heart that as a man disciplines his son, so the LORD your God disciplines you." Deuteronomy 4:36 says "From heaven he made you hear his voice to discipline you. On earth he showed you his great fire, and you heard his words from out of the fire."

According to scripture, discipline brings blessings. Job 5:17: Blessed is the one whom God corrects; so do not despise the discipline of the Almighty. Psalm 94:12: Blessed is the one you discipline, LORD, the one you teach from your law."

PALM TREES AND HURRICANES

It is not "natural" within our carnal man to be disciplined. I, like most people, am not a naturally disciplines person. However, it is my decision to bring myself under control and influence to the Spirit of God. For me, it is a learned behavior that is all about results. I want the result of saying "no" to chocolate cake or "no" to a door that will lead me down a pathway where I don't want to go. I want the result of spending time alone with God. I want the result of planning and ordering my day. We must learn motivation to discipline our own spirit. Paul said it this way, "But I discipline my body and keep it under control, lest after preaching to others I myself should be disqualified" (1 Corinthians 9:27, ESV).

It is a learned lesson. I remember a time in my life when I had been guilty of neglecting my physical temple. I allowed myself to become so overbooked and overextended in ministry events and activities that I became physically exhausted and deathly ill. I developed severe lung problems. Through prayer, rest and medical help, I regained the health of my lungs, but made a commitment to pursue both spiritual and physical wholeness.

I have decided to feed my spirit and body every day. I wake up, meditate, read God's Word, spend time in prayer, and journal. My most important discipline is to spend every morning with God. I also commit to 30 minutes of exercise every day—I use the treadmill or elliptical while reading or listening to God's Word some more. Finally, I make notes of all that I want to accomplish that day. They are habits I have developed for my daily life.

This is my routine every single day and it is so important. Spiritually, I know what I do first has great impact on my entire day. The way I begin my day will determine what dictates my day.

Balance and discipline enable my spirit man to stay strong. So now, when my body starts to break down, I pay attention to the signals it sends me. I'll take the day off, spend time with friends, rest or do something that gives me a mental or emotional break.

Believe it or not, an important ingredient to discipline and inner strength is flexibility. You must learn how to be flexible in life. There was a hurricane in Tampa a few years ago that destroyed a giant oak tree in my yard. The beautiful oak tree split right down the middle. Meanwhile, all around it were rather ugly palm trees. They looked a mess, but they were still standing. The palm trees bent with the extremely high winds, but because palm trees have extraordinarily deep roots, they would not break.

That's how it is in life. You have to be rooted in disciplines. Tell me what a person does daily, and I'll tell you what their future will be like. You grow your roots every day by the actions you take. Don't wait until you get in a crisis to build an ark. Learn to build and prepare through daily disciplines—spiritually, emotionally, mentally, and physically.

DISCIPLINE . . . AND SO MUCH MORE

The concept of discipline is related to a key scripture, 2 Timothy 1:7, "For God hath not given us the spirit of fear; but of power, and of love, and of a sound mind." I believe discipline is an important principle to embrace that will allow you to experience wholeness in mind, body, soul and spirit.

God does not view you as only a spiritual being, but sees you as a whole, complete person. And He wants you to live a quality life spiritually, emotionally and physically. As the Master Creator, God's plan for you is to live with balance, success and joy.

As part of God's perfect plan for your life, there are some important truths that I have learned over the years:

•   God has an overall set of principles that produce the best possible health for each person.

•   You are responsible for setting priorities and establishing the habits of your own life.

•   Higher quality decisions produce a higher quality life.

Discipline comes down to your decisions. And decisions determine your destiny. It is said that great people do daily what others do occasionally. You must make decisions based on what you are willing to cut out of or add to your life for a desired end result.

Daniel:
I believe that the Old Testament's Daniel is probably one of the most disciplined individuals in God's Word. As a young man, Daniel was among those captured by Nebuchadnezzar, king of Babylon, to serve in his court. These chosen servants were to eat and drink from the "royal menu" and be treated well. But Daniel was so disciplined in God's commands for living that he refused to eat the king's royal food and wine. Instead, Daniel and a few others worked out a deal with the guard who was in charge of them.

"Please test your servants for ten days, and let them give us vegetables to eat and water to drink. Then, let our appearance be examined before you, and the appearance of the young men who eat the portion of the king's delicacies; and as you see fit, so deal with your servants" (Daniel 1:12-13, NKJV).

It was a contest to see who had better health, Daniel and those fasting before the Lord or the others who ate meat and drank wine. At the end of the time, Daniel and friends "appeared better and fatter in flesh than all the young men who ate the portion of the king's delicacies" (Daniel 1:15, NKJV). Daniel and his men were healthier because they maintained their discipline to eating and drinking only what God commanded. Discipline brings rewards.

Daniel is also the one who made it a practice to pray to God three times a day, regardless of his situation. In Daniel 6, his political enemies conspired to turn the king against him. They tricked the king into making it a crime to pray to anyone but the king.

Even though Daniel knew the punishment was death in the lion's den, he never faltered in his time with God. "Now when Daniel learned that the decree had been published, he went home to his upstairs room where the windows opened toward Jerusalem. Three times a day he got down on his knees and prayed, giving thanks to his God, just as he had done before" (Daniel 6:10, NIV).

For staying faithful to his discipline of prayer, Daniel was arrested and thrown into a pit with hungry lions. But God had a plan.

"At the first light of dawn, the king got up and hurried to the lions' den. When he came near the den, he called to Daniel in an anguished voice, 'Daniel, servant of the living God, has your God, whom you serve continually, been able to rescue you from the lions?' Daniel answered, 'May the king live forever! My God sent his angel, and he shut the mouths of the lions. They have not hurt me, because I was found innocent in his sight. Nor have I ever done any wrong before you, Your Majesty.' The king was overjoyed and gave orders to lift Daniel out of the den. And when Daniel was lifted from the den, no wound was found on him, because he had trusted in his God" (Daniel 6:19- 23).

I believe when we stay faithful to God in our disciplines He can do miraculous things in our life even when it does not appear to be that way for a season. Stay faithful during the times of testing.

LIVING WITH DISCIPLINE DAILY

One of the best definitions I've ever heard of willpower for the Christian is this: Willpower is MY will and GOD'S POWER. God cares about your health and physical well-being. He cares about your emotional and spiritual well-being. He cares about your needs and desires. God's Word emphasizes wholeness. God wants you to live in a harmonious wellness that covers your body, mind, emotions, spirit, and all of your relationships. There's no part of your being that God leaves out. He sees you as a whole and He moves continually to make you whole. But I believe it all starts with discipline. The Word of God reminds us in 1 Samuel 15:22 that "to obey is better than sacrifice."

SET REALISTIC GOALS.

Once you determine what area of your life needs more discipline, take the time to think it through. Set daily goals, weekly goals, monthly goals and beyond. These must be realistic goals you can achieve. Consistency is the key to discipline. Make sure you commit to accomplishing those goals every single day, just one step at a time.

BELIEVE THAT YOU CAN DO IT AND START WITH THE FIRST STEP.

Jesus said a grain of mustard seed was enough to yield big results (Matthew17: 20). I believe the same can be true when you decide to live a more disciplined life. Take it one step at a time. Start where you are and take it one day at a time if you need to. Plan your day today to include a time of quiet and prayer. Eat a healthy breakfast today. Go for a walk today. Go by the university admissions office to pick up an application today. You have to start sometime, why not today?

ASK GOD TO HELP YOU.

Learn to yield certain habits to God. Pray daily (hourly if you have too!) for strength to overcome temptation. Find a few of your favorite scripture verses to read when you struggle with making the right decisions.

Practical steps to "discipline"

Choose an area of your life to practice more discipline. Set some daily goals. Keep a journal of your progress. Reward yourself for achievement.

REFLECTIONS

Why is discipline important in our lives?

_____
_____
_____
_____
_____
_____

What has been the worst area of discipline in your life?

_____
_____
_____
_____
_____
_____

How has that specific area affected your life over the years?

_____
_____
_____
_____

Now create a detailed list of every area you need more discipline.

How many bible verses on "discipline" can you find? Write them down, place them in specific places, and read them daily.

Set time aside and just talk to God about your life, your weaknesses, your concerns.

What can you do to help others understand DISCIPLINE?

chapter six: **accountability**

"The currency of the Kingdom is relationship."

L et me ask you a question—who is next to you? It's really a question about accountability, another powerful word that has transformed my life. Who are you accountable to? To be accountable for someone means the quality or state of being accountable; especially an obligation or willingness to accept responsibility or to account for one's actions. To be accountable to means subject to giving an account, or answer, to.

Accountability goes up and down. Who are you accountable to? Who, and what are you accountable for? These are important questions. As children of God, we are all accountable to God. But He has also placed people in our lives who can keep us heading in the right direction. It is through community and connection that we grow, develop, are built in love and find safety. One of the fundamental needs in all people is to be "safe"—to have a genuine connection with a mutual give- and-take of caring that flows between individuals where both people bring their lives, loves, joys and sorrows to the connection.

SPIRITUAL DADDY AND MOMMA

I've been blessed to be advised and guided by mighty men and women of God who taught me the lesson of accountability. God has used these relationships to help transform me through humility and mentorship. By learning to submit my life to someone in a role of Christian mentorship in my life, I have been covered by that person's good standing with God through Christ.

We are all influenced by the people God has placed in our lives. But there are those who come into our lives with the God-given assignment of mentorship and/or authority. You have to have someone in your life that you can really hold yourself accountable to . . . for me it's been my spiritual mother and father, and I give God the glory for bringing them into my life. In fact, I do not make any major life decision consciously without seeking the counsel of my spiritual "covering."

I remember one time when their influence was particularly important. I was working out a publishing agreement for my first major book. I considered two different publishing houses, but really had my mind set on one. My spiritual father advised me to choose the other one. I spent a little time trying to convince him on my first choice. But, in the end, I submitted myself to his wisdom and followed his advice. It was a good choice. To this day, that book is still my number one best seller! God will honor when you obey.

THE POWER OF NEXT

By answering the question, "who is next to you," you say a lot about your life and your future. The power of next is the value of building accountability relationships on respect, loyalty, and trust through inspiration and motivation. The people in your life— those you "stand next to"—reveal a lot about your own faith, passion and vision. Not only do those next to you help reveal your own ambitions and passions, but through the power of next they can help you achieve your God-given dreams.

The "power of next" can:

- Help you rebuild what the enemy has torn down.

- Give you encouragement and focus.

- Help you find wholeness and healing.

- Accelerate your God-given destiny.

In the Old Testament, Nehemiah used the power of next to achieve God's purpose and plan. He was given a divine assignment by God to rebuild the walls of Jerusalem, which had been torn down by the enemy. He accomplished in 52 days what no one had been able to do in 90 years—rebuild the walls. The key? Relationships. Nehemiah knew he could not accomplish the task alone.

Read in Nehemiah 3 about the process of rebuilding the walls. "Then Eliashib the high priest rose up with his brethren the priests and built the Sheep Gate; they consecrated it and hung its doors. They built as far as the Tower of the Hundred, and consecrated it, then as far as the Tower of Hananel. Next to Eliashib the men of Jericho built. And next to them Zaccur the son of Imri built . . . And so on. . ." (Nehemiah 3:1-9, NKJV).

The world "next" is used 16 times in Nehemiah 3. The chapter is full of the names of people who shared Nehemiah's vision and made it happen. Teamwork is the ability to work together—or next to each other—for common vision.

"Can two walk together, unless they are agreed?" (Amos 3:3, NKJV). It is all about accountability with those you are "next to."

Accountability leads to the Principle of Know. God wants us to know those He has placed in our life profoundly, intimately. The key is to look past the exterior and get to know the real person. Never stop seeking to know each other. Pay close attention to the details and don't take each other for granted. Knowledge is a lifelong process.

When you get "Next" to others and "Know" others, you can begin to rebuild the walls of abandonment, isolation, anger, pain, and abuse. Through this critical principle of accountability, you can move into the wholeness God has planned for your life.

SHUNAMMITE WOMAN: CONNECTION

We are all anointed for a purpose, purely ordained by God. There is a call on your life. But God must first cultivate you. So God places people in your life that can help release His glory and take you to the next level . . . these are partnerships of accountability.

To unlock your spiritual potential, you need that partnership. When God wants to bless you, He sends a person into your life. The people in your life determine where you are going and how you are going to get there. God works through people.

One of the most powerful examples of that can be found in II Kings 4:8-9: "And it fell on a day that Elijah passed to Shunem where there was a great woman and she constrained him to eat bread and so it was that as oft as he passed by he turned into there to eat bread and she said unto her husband behold now I perceive that this is a holy man of God who passes by us continually."

There are three aspects of this story you need to understand to unlock the greatness inside of you through accountability:
1. 1.   Her Potential.
The Bible calls the Shunammite woman "great" before anything happened in her life. Later in the Word, we see her great faith that brought miracles into her life. But God called her great out of her potential. You have potential, too. When God speaks to you, He doesn't

see your current state. He speaks to you from your future.

But to release that potential, God takes you through a process. . . and part of the process is for you to connect with people God has placed in your life for partnership, mentorship and accountability. These connections release your potential and the greatness on the inside of you.

To release her potential, the Shunammite woman had to see it ... she had to sow into it ... and she had to seal it. She saw the greatness she wanted in Elijah. She wanted to be connected to Elijah's anointing, to his covenant and position with God. When Elijah passed by, the Bible says this woman constrained him. She reached out and grabbed her opportunity. She was not going to miss her moment!

After she saw the greatness, the Shunammite woman sowed into it by making a provision, a shelter for Elijah. Sowing is more than money—it is praying, serving, laboring in the spirit. What you sow into is what you have a right to receive. The Shunammite woman sealed her faith because she saw it and sowed into it!

1. 2.   His Position.
"Remember them which have the rule over you who have spoken unto the word of God whose faith follow considering the end of their conversation" (Hebrews 13:7).

The Shunammite woman saw an opportunity to learn and receive impartation from Elijah. She followed his faith. You need to connect with a spiritual authority. Position yourself with the anointed people of God. Know that all who are called by God have both a divinity and humanity side. There is no perfect person but Jesus. God is the One who ordains their position of authority and as I honor that authority I honor God. Anointed people are individuals who draw us closer to being the people God intended us to be. Though not perfect, they are "good enough in their own character that the net effect of their presence in our lives is positive. You will be great as you honor those God has placed in leadership over your life. You are commanded to follow the faith!

1. 3. Their promise.

The relationship of Elijah and the Shunammite woman released the miraculous power of the Spirit. Together, they unlocked God's promise of greatness. You can do the same. Your promise of greatness will be released as you realize your potential submitting yourself to be accountable to someone God has positioned in your life.

APPLYING ACCOUNTABILITY

Your life is a picture of those around you. Whoever stands next to you day in and day out says a lot about who you are. So look around . . . consider those closest to you . . . and take a closer examination of your relationships.

For accountability, you must be near or close to someone. And when you are close, there is contact! With contact, there is impartation. Whoever you are close to flows into you. There is a connection. Where there is a connection, there is access and influence or power. You become a product of who or what you are next to for good or bad. "Do not be deceived: 'Evil company corrupts good habits'" (1 Corinthians 15:33, NKJV). "He who walks with wise men will be wise, But the companion of fools will be destroyed" (Proverbs 13:20, NKJV).

So be careful about who you associate and fellowship with in your everyday life. Make sure their actions portray the principles and belief system you want for your life. There are those assigned to be next to you with accountability, after you and before you. When all three positions are functioning in your life, you will experience wholeness. Practical steps to "accountability"

Join a local church and attend regularly.

Find an accountability partner who is a greater spiritual authority. Meet regularly with your accountability partner.

REFLECTIONS

Why is accountability important?

_____
_____
_____
_____
_____
_____

What are some important areas to have accountability in?

_____
_____
_____
_____
_____
_____

How does a lack of accountability negatively impact yourself and others?

_____
_____
_____
_____
_____
_____

How does accountability help yourself and others?

_____
_____
_____
_____
_____
_____

Who are the people who have most influenced your life so far?

_____

_____

_____

_____

_____

Who are the people you need to be accountable to? How does that help you?

_____

_____

_____

_____

_____

_____

Write out a plan to improve on your accountability.

_____

_____

_____

_____

_____

_____

Who is accountable to you? How will you help them?

_____

_____

_____

_____

_____

_____

What can you do to help others understand ACCOUNTABILITY?

_____

_____

_____

_____

_____

_____

chapter seven: **courage**

> "Courage is the resistance to fear not the absence of fear."

On January 8, 2011, Tucson, Arizona, became a place of tragedy and heartbreak. Six people, including a 9-year-old girl, died during a shooting rampage at a political event. Thirteen others were wounded, including U.S. Rep. Gabrielle Giffords, who was left fighting for her life.

But Arizona was also a place of courage that day. Bystanders did things they never imagined they could . . . while under fire.

A 74-year-old retired Army colonel, wounded by one of the bullets sprayed into the crowd, pulled the gunman to the ground while others helped jump on the attacker and held him down. A 61- year-old woman grabbed a fresh magazine the gunman was reaching for to reload. And a 20-year-old college student used his bare hands at first to try and stop the bleeding from Rep. Giffords' critical head wound.

These heroes defined courage in that moment. I have no doubt they were afraid. Courage is the resistance to fear and the mastery of fear, not the absence of fear. Each one made the choice to act with courage, despite the danger.

Courage, a life-changing and life-saving word, is key to overcoming every battle in life. Courage is the quality of mind or spirit that enables a person to face difficulties, danger, pain and more without fear. It is bravery. The most useful and transformational experiences I've ever had demanded that I choose courage. When you know how to act with courage, it can transform your life.

I CAME OUT FIGHTING

I often joke that on the day I was born, I came out fighting. . . and have been fighting ever since. It was not by personal choice or decision. I was born breach with the umbilical cord wrapped around my neck. Since that day, overcoming through God-given courage has been the overarching theme of my life.

It wasn't something I chose. But because of the physical and sexual abused I endured as a child, fear and anxiety was a constant that I had to face and overcome. Statistics said I would have addiction issues and most likely be institutionalized or jailed by adulthood and there would be a greater propensity to further victimization in adulthood.

I was pregnant by age 18 and the future looked bleak. The conditions of my life were so severe that I should have never been able to overcome. All the conditions were ripe for failure. But when I found God, His courage took root in my heart as His love began to heal me..

The fighting didn't end after I got saved. When I started in the ministry, I didn't look the part, according to the standards of man. I didn't have the right background or picture perfect life. I should have failed. But God had a plan. He gave me the courage to stand in the face of the doubts and fear of man's opinion and adverse circumstances.

I chose to overcome by listening to the voice of God and letting it be louder than any other in my life. And I didn't just hear His voice, I let it work in me. In my weakness, His strength has been made perfect and we are more than conquerors through Christ Jesus!

You have to fasten to hope, to courage, to God's Word and what He says about you. Most of what I've done, I've done in the face of fear. And I'm not super confident in myself, but I am in God. He is my anchor, my rock and solid foundation. That is when I have learned to stand for strength.

INGREDIENTS FOR COURAGE

Understanding how to live and walk with courage can make a big difference in your life and in what you accomplish for God. We can see some of the ingredients we need for the courage to overcome the trials in our own lives by studying David's actions at Ziklag.

"And it came to pass, when David and his men were come to Ziklag on the third day, that the Amalekites had invaded the south, and Ziklag, and smitten Ziklag, and burned it with fire; And had taken the women captives, that were therein: they slew not any, either great or small, but carried them away, and went on their way. So David and his men came to the city, and, behold, it was burned with fire; and their wives, and their sons, and their daughters, were taken captives" (1 Samuel 30:1-3).

• Courage needs a crisis.
A terrible crisis, an injustice has happened in David's life. His home has been attacked and burned to the ground and his family taken. David wasn't just facing a loss, he was facing devastation.

I want you to understand that courage can only rise to the top in times of crisis. Don't curse your crisis. The problems we face grow and strengthen our faith and resolve. You wouldn't be the person you are today without the trials you have endured and overcome! You cannot conquer without conflict. You cannot win without a war. The tragic conditions David faced were ripe for courage.

• Courage needs honest emotions.
"Then David and the people that were with him lifted up their voice and wept, until they had no more power to weep. And David was greatly distressed; for the people spake of stoning him, because the soul of all the people was grieved, every man for his sons and for his daughters" (1 Samuel 30:4, 6).

Before David did anything, he grieved. He expressed his anguish, fear and pain. You always see David's humanity before his spirituality. Let me tell you this, courage is not about preventing fear and doubt from coming into your life. They will come. Courage is about moving beyond that fear.

It is okay to experience the emotions of fear and pain. It is okay to cry. In fact you need to because that is part of the process. God made us to do that. Tears have a language of their own that speaks to the heart of God. He can interpret the pain you cannot articulate. So express your grief or fear . . . but just don't camp out there. Know that you have hope beyond the tragedy and pain.

• Courage needs encouragement.
After he grieved, Scripture says, "but David encouraged himself in the LORD his God." (1 Samuel 30:6). In Hebrew, the word "encouraged" is to fasten onto, to seize, to help oneself. David reached out beyond his despair and discouragement to help himself through God's courage. David locked onto courage!

As David "encouraged" himself, he "fastened to hope." Proverbs 13:12 says, "Hope deferred makes the heart sick, but a longing fulfilled is a tree of life." Courage is hope! It's what God says to you in the face of all appearances.
David knew how to encourage himself and others through God's promises. "And David said to Solomon his son, Be strong and of good

courage, and do it; fear not, nor be dismayed: for the LORD God, even my God will be with thee; he will not fail thee, nor forsake thee, until thou has finished all the work for the service of the house of the LORD" (1 Chronicles 28:20).

When you face an uphill battle, encourage yourself. Ephesians 5:19 says, "Speaking to yourself in psalms and hymns and spiritual songs, singing and making melody in your heart to the Lord." Believe in what God can do through you. "I can do all things through Christ which strengtheneth me" (Philippians 4:13). Encourage has the root word "Coeur" in the romance languages, which means "heart." When you encourage, you add to someone's heart.

• Courage needs patience.
Sometimes you have to wait for an answer to prayer or for direction. Waiting on God takes courage. But it is in the waiting that your courage will grow. Psalm 27:14 says, "Wait on the LORD: be of good courage, and he shall strengthen thine heart: wait, I say, on the LORD."

• Courage needs God's guidance.
Before David pursued the enemy he asked for God's direction. "And David inquired at the LORD, saying, Shall I pursue after this troop? Shall I overtake them? And he answered him, Pursue; for thou shalt surely overtake them, and without fail recover all" (1 Samuel 30:8). When you face a crisis, turn and face God. Ask Him for wisdom and guidance. He will provide it.

God acts, he doesn't react. He is the Master Strategist. Therefore, you must be led by His Spirit to be successful. Seek the Lord. David didn't even ask for recovery, he just asked if he should pursue the enemy. When you seek courage and have the patience to wait for it, God will always give you more than you ask for.

• Courage needs action.
I love how Scripture simply says, "So David went . . ." (1 Samuel 30:9). There was no hesitation or discussion. God told David to pursue

and David pursued. When God tells you to go . . . GO! "Now the kingdom of heaven suffereth violence and the violent take it by force . . ." (Matthew 11:12). Don't let anything stand in your way when you get the green light.

Do not be afraid to go for it. Romans 8:31 says, "What shall we then say to these things? If God be for us, who can be against us?" When God instructs you to pursue, expect that you will recover whatever the enemy has stolen—peace, financial security, joy, good health, family and more!

LIVING WITH COURAGE

Through your courage, God makes the impossible possible. I began this chapter with the story of individuals who showed remarkable courage during a great tragedy on January 8, 2011 in Tucson, Arizona. Because they took action in the face of adversity, they saved lives. But they were not the only ones who exhibited courage that day. Shooting victim U.S. Rep. Gabrielle Giffords began a courageous fight for her life that day.

Her husband, NASA astronaut Mark Kelly told participants at the National Prayer Breakfast a month after the shooting that his renewed faith helped give him courage during the most difficult time of his life. He said, "I thought the world just spins and the clock just ticks and things happen for no particular reason. But from space, far above that traffic on the New Jersey turnpike, you have an entirely different perspective of life on our planet. It's humbling to see the earth as God created it in the context of God's vast universe. God bless you and please continue to keep Gabby's thoughts and prayers in your heart. It is really helping."

Knowing we have the God of the universe on our side inspires courage. Praying for His guidance and strength is essential to living a life of courage. Rep. Giffords was shot at point blank range in the head . . . she wasn't supposed to live that day. But then God's people began to pray and changed the story. Rep. Giffords is a living, breathing example of how courage can make the impossible possible.

Practical steps to "courage"

Find encouraging Scriptures in God's Word. Pray and ask for God's strength and guidance. Take action.

REFLECTIONS

Define courage.

_____
_____
_____
_____
_____
_____
_____

How many bible verses on courage can you find? Write them down.

_____
_____
_____
_____
_____
_____
_____

What are your greatest fears in life?

_____
_____
_____
_____
_____
_____
_____

What are some misconceptions about "courage"?

_____

_____
_____
_____
_____
_____
_____

What needs do you have in your life that require courage? What specific goals will be accomplished?

_____
_____
_____
_____
_____
_____
_____

How has the enemy hindered and manipulated you to limit your courage?

_____
_____
_____
_____
_____
_____
_____

What can you do to help others understand COURAGE?

_____
_____
_____
_____
_____
_____
_____

chapter eight: **perseverance**

"Great people are not people who have everything
go right; they are people who refuse to quit."

President Calvin Coolidge once said, "Nothing in this world can
take the place of persistence. Talent will not; nothing is more
common than unsuccessful men with talent. Genius will not;
unrewarded genius is almost a proverb. Education will not; the world
is full of educated derelicts. Persistence and determination alone are
omnipotent."

The word "perseverance" makes the difference in life. Coolidge knew
a lot about the concept. His mother died when he was 12 years old
and his sister died at age 15, when Coolidge was 18. Yet Coolidge
persevered. Tragedy surfaced again later in his life. While he was
running for the presidency in 1924, his son died. Again he persevered.
He refused to quit and allowed trouble to become his incubator for
greatness.

Everyone will face tragedy and trials at one point or another. Perseverance separates winners from losers. To persevere is to continue steadfastly or with determination, to be stationary and steadfast, to have fortitude. He that perseveres makes difficulties advancement and contests victory. Those who keep moving forward in the face of defeat will find victory. Great people are not people who have everything go right, they are people who refuse to quit.

Often, what we obtain too easily we value too lightly. The cost of something gives it value and appreciation.

I WILL NEVER GIVE UP!

I have learned that if I really want something I know God has for me, I must say, "I'll never give up" and persevere in the face of all obstacles. Perseverance is vital for transformation! Perseverance means that you must go on resolutely or stubbornly in spite of opposition, importunity, or warning. You must be insistent in the repetition or pressing of an utterance. You must follow your plan of action all the way through . . . and often continue on a set path well past a usual, expected, or normal time.

Perseverance is to stand firm under pressure, to go on resolutely or even stubbornly with a plan to achieve a goal or destination— in spite of opposition, importunity, or warning!

The truth is that there is always opposition to anything you are believing God to fulfill in your life. In fact, trouble or created tension becomes the catalyst for your faith to function! "Falling down" is not failure or an indictment of your capacities! "Staying down" is. Sir Winston Churchill famously said "Success is going from failure to failure without losing enthusiasm."

Each setback in my life has given me experience to draw on—from the abuse and pain of childhood to the devastation of divorce, the loss of a child, 18 life crises, and tragedy as an adult. To persevere means to see through the trouble. You must have the perspective of "heaven" when you are going through "hell." Perseverance helped me keep going. Too many people start goals and never finish. Staying power is important, and only you can determine how important your goal or destination is to you… and how long you intend to pursue it.

THE SYROPHENICIAN WOMAN: NOTHING PERSONAL

Matthew 15:21-28 tells of a woman of Canaan – Syrophenician – who came to Jesus asking, "Lord help me!" She had a sick child at home possessed by a devil. Even though the disciples told her to go away, she wouldn't give up. She persevered with her goal—to get Jesus to go home with her to heal her child.

At first, Jesus ignored her. She would not go away. Jesus' disciples became agitated and asked Him to send her away. Jesus told the woman that He was only sent to the Jews and couldn't help her. She would not go away . . . and may have gotten even louder.

Jesus made a statement that would have sent most people running with an attitude when He said, "It is not meet to take the children's bread, and to cast it to dogs" (Matthew 15:26). This woman stayed and kept pursuing Him.

His harsh words did not even phase the woman. "And she said, 'Truth, Lord: yet the dogs eat of the crumbs which fall from their masters' table' " (Matthew 15:27). That's persistence! Jesus was deeply moved by her faith and tenacity.

"Then Jesus answered and said to her, 'O woman, great is your faith: be it to you even as you will.' And her daughter was made whole from that very hour" (Matthew 15:28). The Syrophenician woman's persistence paid off. She achieved her goal and desire because she never gave up. Like the Syrophenician woman, your tenacious, relentless faith will touch the heart of God.

LIVING IN PERSEVERANCE

Like the Syrophenician woman, are you too desperate to be denied by God? How do you persevere? Put these practical tips for perseverance into action.

REMEMBER HOW YOU MADE IT THROUGH OTHER TIMES OF STRUGGLE AND STRIFE IN YOUR LIFE. "But call to remembrance the former days, in which, after ye were illuminated, ye endured a great fight of afflictions; Partly, whilst ye were made a gazingstock both by reproaches and afflictions; and partly, whilst ye became companions of them that were so used. For ye had compassion of me in my bonds, and took joyfully the spoiling of your goods, knowing in yourselves that ye have in heaven a better and an enduring substance" (Hebrews 10:32-34).

HAVE CONFIDENCE AND ASSURANCE THAT GOD WANTS WHAT'S BEST FOR YOU AND HAS THE POWER TO SEE YOU THROUGH. "Being confident of this very thing, that he which hath begun a good work in you will perform it until the day of Jesus Christ" (Philippians 1:6).

REALIZE THAT THERE IS A PURPOSE TO YOUR STRUGGLE. Everybody has a storm. Life is fair and we all go through trials. But there is a purpose to your pain. God is directing your destiny and He is the God of your storm. It might not be "God-sent" but it will be "God-used."

FIND GOD'S PRESENCE IN YOUR TRIAL. There is nothing that you will ever go through that God is not with you—"I am with you always, even to the end of the age" (Matthew 28:20). Where His presence is, there is provision and protection.

UNDERSTAND THE POWER OF GOD IN THE STORM. God invests in you when you are down. "He gives power to the weak, and to those who have no might He increases strength" (Isaiah 40:29). In your trial, you can see His greatness. God can speak peace to your storm … shut the lion's mouth … and shield you from the fiery furnace!

LET THE HOLY SPIRIT GIVE YOU PEACE AND A CALMNESS. The enemy wants to fill you with anxiety and keep you from accomplishing all that God has planned for your life. So, no matter what trials the devil throws at you, keep your focus on God. Stand your ground in calm assurance that He is working in your best interest. ". . . and having done all, to stand, stand therefore," (Ephesians 6:13).

Think with the mind of God. When you start thinking about God, your life will line up with the plan of God. Ask God to give you His eyes of understanding. I stand on James 1:5 every day of my life: "if any of you lacks wisdom, let him ask of God, who gives to all liberally and without reproach, and it will be given to him."

GUARD HOW YOU FEEL ABOUT THINGS. It is not what you go through, but how you go through it that matters. Do you respond or react? How does it affect you? Remember that your body is world- conscious. Your mind is self-conscious and your spirit is God-conscious. The one that you feed will grow and govern your feelings and thoughts.

Practical steps to "perseverance"

Bind the Word of God to your heart. Take on a confident attitude. Associate with victors, not victims. Remind your enemy of his defeat.

REFLECTIONS

Define perseverance.

_____

_____

_____

_____

_____

_____

_____

_____

_____

How has a lack of perseverance held you back up to this point?

What are some strategies to help you overcome tragedies and focus on God?

_____

_____

_____

_____

_____

_____

_____

Do you have any favorite biblical characters who exhibited perseverance? What can you learn from them?

_____

_____

_____

_____

_____

_____

_____

What does the bible say about perseverance? Write it down to look at daily!

_____

_____

_____

_____

_____

_____

Write out a list of specific ways you will persevere from today on.

_____

_____

_____

_____

_____

_____

_____

Write down scriptures that will help you persevere

_____

_____

_____

_____

_____

_____

_____

What can you do to help others understand PERSEVERANCE?

_____

_____

_____

_____

_____

_____

_____

chapter nine: **forgiveness**

"Forgiveness brings you freedom."

What has God brought you from? Where were you when He reached down with His mighty hand of grace and deliverance to lift you out of the mess that you were in? When I stop to really think about my own salvation . . . I mean really think about what it means, I feel the power of freedom! And freedom starts with one word—forgiveness. I'm talking about forgiveness from God as well as forgiveness for others. It also includes forgiving myself for the past. Forgiveness is a principle that has truly transformed my life and allowed me to live in freedom and purpose. I know it can do the same for you.

Maybe you've been to hell and back. Maybe the enemy didn't want to let you go. It doesn't matter. You wouldn't be reading this book if God had not touched you. And it doesn't matter where you've been or what you've done, God has big plans for your life. He wants to make you a living testament of His power to the world. God saved you and has a purpose for your life. It all begins with His forgiveness and love for you.

One thing I know . . . at some point in your life you will be hurt and betrayed by another. It is a reality. Jesus told His disciples in Luke 17:1, "It is impossible but that offenses must come." But He commands them to forgive "seven times a day" if the offender repents. And His disciples responded, "Lord, increase my faith." Your forgiveness has to do with your faith. A high level of faith equals a high level of forgiveness and vice versa.

Our ability to forgive is also tied to our ability to be blessed. Mark 11:24-26 says, "Therefore, I say unto you, What things soever ye desire, when ye pray, believe that you receive them, and ye shall have them." And when ye stand praying—forgive, if ye have ought against any that your Father also which is in heaven may forgive you your trespasses. But if you do not forgive, neither will your Father which is in heaven forgive your trespasses."

Forgiveness brings liberation to you!

THE LITTLE GIRL IN ME
Through my many trials over the years, God taught me that forgiveness includes giving myself permission to be human and learning how to forgive myself. Forgiveness means forgiving others so that I can move past . . . my past.

One day, many years ago, when I was working with inner city children in Washington, D.C., I remember one little girl that came in on the bus ministry who had obvious signs of abuse. She was tattered and torn. I grabbed another worker to help her immediately and then fled to the back where I cried my eyes out. It was too familiar to me.

I was that broken little girl! I cried out to God, "I cannot do this!" It was like I was looking at myself in that little girl. I said, "I can't forgive them. I can't do it." It stirred up so many emotions about the pain and abuse I had suffered from sexual and physical abuse from the time I was age 6 to 13.

When I cried out, "I can't do this," I felt the voice of God in my spirit—His Holy Spirit spoke
inside me, saying, "I know you can't. You've been trying within your own strength and power. If you allow me to place forgiveness in you... you can release them."

The love of God is brought about by the Holy Spirit. If God can place love in our hearts, He can place forgiveness there as well. The day I asked the Spirit to place forgiveness in my heart, suddenly there was a liberty in my spirit... I was free. Although I still had knowledge of what happened to me, I had no association with the pain. Instead, it had turned to compassion. I saw it differently. It's called loving someone with "agape" love—the love of God for and with humans, humanity, who can potentially hurt you and harm you.

You make the decision to give them the gift of love. My part to play in forgiveness is saying, "I can't forgive—but God can place forgiveness in me." It was a critical lesson. Without it, I would not have been able to follow God's complete destiny for my life. I would have been emotionally stuck in the past and a victim to all that I had been through. You cannot make a mark until God has your heart. He is about to heal everywhere you have been hurt.

THE ADULTEROUS WOMAN: STUCK IN THE PAST
Your level of faith impacts your level of forgiveness . . . which also impacts your level of love . .
. and your future. It reminds me of Ham in Genesis 9:22; his father Noah had gotten drunk and fell asleep naked. We are told, "When Ham saw the nakedness of his father, he went and told his two brothers. But the two boys, (Shem and Japheth) took a sheet and covered their father."

FORGIVENESS AND LOVE WILL CAUSE YOU TO COVER ANOTHER PERSON'S NAKEDNESS. WHAT WAS THE result? In Scripture we see that Ham was cursed, while God blessed Shem and Japheth.

In John 8:1-12, we see another story of forgiveness in action. It is the story of a woman caught in the very act of adultery in John 8:1-12. She was naked, stripped of her dignity and shamed for her sin. Christ's enemies flung her to the ground before Jesus. They interrupted His teaching and demanded to know what He would do with her. Maybe the mistakes of your past have stripped you of your dignity and joy. Maybe people want to hold you to the shame and guilt of bad decisions and things of your past.

When accusers had the woman of John 8 in their clutches, what did Christ do? He bent down and began writing in the sand. I love this explanation: Salvation is God stooping down to reach us in the entanglement of sin. He lowered Himself to earth and became a man so that you and I can experience His forgiveness for our sins.

Jesus asked her, "Woman, where are those accusers of yours? Has no one condemned you?" (John 8:10, NKJV). When she replied, "No one, Lord," then, He spoke these words of peace and freedom to the woman, "Neither do I condemn you; go and sin no more" (John 8:11, NKJV).

Jesus also said, "I am the light of the world: he that follows Me shall not walk in darkness, but shall have the light of life" (John 8:12). Jesus offers you and me the same forgiveness He gave the woman. He stooped down and wrote in the dirty places of her life.

Something that I find interesting, though, is that after her accusers leave, the woman is still "standing in the midst," according to John 8:9. Sometimes after we have encountered forgiveness, we have a hard time moving forward. Maybe you have been there . . . been hurt so bad and for so long, you are still waiting to feel the pain of that first stone. Or maybe you can't forgive yourself or those who have hurt you. You have to take those first steps of forgiveness to experience freedom. It's time to move on and get beyond the trespasses of your yesterday.

LIVING IN FORGIVENESS

I've learned some important steps of forgiveness from Scripture, prayer, God-given mentors, and my own trial and error.

First, remember your own forgiveness. I want to remind you today that God provided life when you were dying, hope when you were hopeless, peace when you were in confusion. He rescued you. He stooped down just in time. He delivered you just in time. You have freedom because of God's forgiveness. It is not something you or I deserved, it is only because of God's love. Because of that grace, God demands that we forgive others. Remember, your faith level has to do with your forgiveness level.

Matthew 5:44 commands you to, "Love your enemies, bless them that curse you, do good to them that hate you, and pray for them, which despitefully use you and persecute you."

Second, you cannot conquer what you will not confront. Unresolved issues are dangerous! The enemy will plant seeds of conflict in your heart to grow and destroy your faith and relationships unless you take immediate action. Resolve issues with a friend or loved one by first identifying and then confronting the problem, large or small. Remember, you can't conquer what you don't confront and you can't confront what you don't identify. Be willing to admit when you are wrong and ask for forgiveness. Forgive others as Christ forgave you. Do not hold bitterness in your heart.

Third, ask for help. Ask God to give you the strength and courage to face your pain and forgive those who have caused you harm. He will be there when you need Him the most. Pray and read His Word. You will find encouraging words to hold on to.
Practical steps to "forgiveness"
Ask God to forgive you of your sins.

Identify the pain in your life that is a stumbling block. Confront and forgive with God's help.
Move on to God's design for your life!

REFLECTIONS

Write out a time when you were hurt by someone you trust.

_____

_____

_____

_____

_____

_____

Tell how Jesus dealt with betrayal. How can you follow His example?

_____

_____

_____

_____

_____

_____

How does unforgiving and bitterness hinder you?

_____

_____

_____

_____

_____

_____

Find every bible verse relating to forgiveness you can and write them down.

_____

_____

_____

_____

_____

_____

_____

Write down a list of everyone you need to forgive or release, and forgive them!

_____

_____

_____

_____

_____

_____

Who needs to forgive you?

_____

_____

_____

_____

_____

_____

How will forgiveness help you?

_____

_____

_____

_____

_____

_____

What can you do to help others understand FORGIVENESS?

_____

_____

_____

_____

_____

_____

chapter ten: **love**

"Love will never fail."

L ove is the ultimate life lesson and the perfect word to conclude our journey of transformation. If condemnation cancels faith, then love activates faith. It is one of the most powerful forces on earth. The desire for love is hardwired into every single person on the face of the earth. Mother Teresa "summed" it up best when she said, "Each person has been created to love and be loved."

Love is the core of our essence, our foundation. We each want to be loved, accepted and respected. Studies have proven that long-term happiness is achieved by the ability to give and receive love, unconditionally. Unconditional love is choosing to love even though there are imperfections that we wish to be other wise. Love is actually a conscious decision that brings wholeness, fulfillment and satisfaction.

The three most important acts of love are:

• LOVING GOD—acknowledging and receiving God's love for you.

• LOVING YOURSELF—you cannot give what you don't have.

• LOVING OTHERS—not only fulfilling but a command of God.

Your "faith" will not work without the proper foundation built on these three manifestations of love. According to 1 Corinthians 13:13, "Faith, hope and love abide; these three but the greatest of these is Love." Faith runs on love. If faith or our foundation is "total trust" then it is grounded or rooted in love.

LOVING GOD
Like the Apostle Paul, my heart's desire is for you "to know the love of Christ which passes knowledge; that you may be filled with all the fullness of God" (Ephesians 3:19). Until you truly know this amazing love, you will never be satisfied and never be fulfilled. It is not a head knowledge, but an intimate relationship born of experience.

I like how the Amplified version of the Bible explains love. Ephesians 3:17-19, "May Christ through your faith (actually) dwell (settle down, abide, make His permanent home) in your hearts! May you be rooted deep in love and founded securely on love; That you may have the power and be strong to apprehend and grasp with all the saints (God's devoted people, the experience of that love) what is the breadth and length and height and depth (of it). [That you may really come to know [practically through experience for yourself], the love of Christ, which far surpasses mere knowledge (without experience), that you may be filled (through all your being) unto all the fullness of God [may have the richest measure of the divine Presence and become a body wholly filled and flooded with God Himself."

LOVING YOURSELF
Throughout this book, I have written about the brokenness and

struggles I dealt with early in life. Those issues made a big difference in how I viewed myself and others. It's not easy to overcome the scars of pain. I had an "empty love tank" because of abandonment and rejection. I had love and relationship issues and because of that I was broken. How about you? Until we can identify that we are frail human beings with flawed mechanisms, we cannot overcome the issue that has us in an undesirable state of being. If you are struggling to accept God's love and, in turn, love yourself, it is a problem with wholeness.

Wholeness occurs when you have a realistic, appreciative, loving opinion of yourself and discern your unconditional human worth. Wholeness tells you that you are important and valuable as a person because your essential, core self is unique, precious, infinite, eternal, of unchanging value and good.

Worth doesn't have to be earned or proved. In fact, the externals of your life neither add nor diminish your worth. You are loveable because God first loved you! And when you are loved, you are fulfilled. While it is wonderful to receive from others, this love, we are not dependent on them when we are plugged into God's love. This is the message Jesus had for the Woman at the Well.

WOMAN AT THE WELL: THIRSTY FOR LOVE
Jesus met a broken women in John 4:1-41 at a well in Samaria. The interaction between the two is one of the greatest analogies of the power of God's love to bring wholeness and satisfaction to an individual.

When Jesus asked the woman for a drink of water, she questioned why He would speak to her, a Samaritan. Jesus reply, "If you knew the gift of God, and who it is that says to you, Give Me to drink; you would have asked of Him, and He would have given you living water" (John 4:10, NKJV).

Jesus was telling the woman that for the real thirst of her heart and soul, she had been drinking from the wrong well (five husbands and a live-in lover). He told her she was trying to fill her desire for love, but that the only true satisfaction came from an intimate relationship with God.

"Whosoever drinks of this water shall thirst again; But whosoever drinks of the water that I shall give him shall never thirst; but the water that I shall give him shall be in him a well of water springing up into everlasting life" (John 4:13-14).

I want to challenge you to change your well – your source of provision. The love you get from others is more likely a reflection of how they feel about themselves, not a reflection of your core worth. No psychological health is possible unless the "essential core" is met, that is to be accepted, loved, and respected.

God's love heals and provides the foundation for growth. In Jeremiah 31:3-4, God declares to you: "Yea, I have loved thee with an everlasting love; therefore, with loving kindness have I drawn thee. Again, I will build thee and thou shalt be built." Only God can build every broken place in your life by His love. Trust Him to heal your past pain.

LOVING OTHERS

Once you accept God's love, grow your love for Him and let Him bring you wholeness and a love for yourself, you are ready to love others. Here are some definitions of love to help you understand its impact on relationships. Love is:

• A feeling that you experience.

• An attitude you act on. Love wants what's best for the loved one at each moment.

• A decision and commitment that you make every day. It can be difficult at times. Sometimes you must "will yourself to love."

• A skill that is cultivated.

Loving is something we learn to do that can be accomplished when you hear the Word, receive the Word, and carry the Word. 1 Corinthians 13 says love endures, is kind, envies not, is not puffed up, does not behave unseemly, is not easily provoked, seeks not her own, thinks no evil, rejoices in truth, bears all things, believes all things, hopes all things, endures all things, and never fails. Love is the foundation to a successful walk of life, faith, and satisfying relationship.

LIVING IN LOVE
Make the decision that you will walk out a life of love daily. Try these practical steps to put love into action in your life.

LOVING GOD ACTION POINTS
For greater love and intimacy with God consider these quick notes from Paul's letter to the Ephesians:

• ". . . do not lose heart at my tribulations for you" (Ephesians 3:13). God has not promised that you will not go through trials, but that He will work them out for your good in the end. Trust that He is on your side.

• ". . . I bow my knees to the Father of our Lord Jesus Christ" (Ephesians 3:14). Approach God in humbleness and prayer. Tear down your walls of self-sufficiency and rest in His provision.

• ". . . strengthened with might through His Spirit in the inner man" (Ephesians 3:16). The Word will perfect the love and strength of God in your life.
Learn to walk in His Spirit and tap into the hidden treasure found through the Holy Spirit.

• ". . . being rooted and grounded in love" (Ephesians 3:17). Most of us are sprinters in life. If you are going to grow, you need to be planted, rooted. The person who endures and stands firm in Christ's love receives the reward.

LOVING YOURSELF ACTION POINTS

For many years, I lost myself in chaos and confusion, trying to fill my desperate need for love. What I did not realize then was that love has nothing to do with what other people do. Love is about wholeness and healing from God. It is about loving yourself. And it is about learning how to connect with people who are safe and supportive of who God intends me to be.

• Acknowledge God's love for you. You never have to face anything alone. The Lord will never leave you, forsake you or abandon you. "For I am persuaded that neither death nor life, nor angels nor principalities nor powers, nor things present nor things to come, nor height nor depth, nor any other created thing, shall be able to separate us from the love of God which is in Christ Jesus our Lord" (Romans 8:38-39). You cannot have self-love if you don't have God love . . . and you cannot love others until you love yourself. Wholeness comes from acceptance and acknowledgement, first from God's love for you and then from loving yourself.

• Work through the layers. There are layers of emotions and feelings that sabotage your relationships and connections. You may have fear associated with guilt and shame. Maybe you've been violated instead of valued. It is only when you admit to and become aware of these feelings that you can tap into your underlying needs and get satisfied in your soul.

• Only you can fix you. Everything in your life is a reflection of your thought process. No one has to punish you in life . . . you punish yourself. The enemy may set up life events to wound you and create negative beliefs about yourself. But no one can make you bitter. No one can make you angry. Your behavior is simply fruit of the root. It comes from your belief system. Likewise, no one else can fix you or complete you. Through a revelation of God's love, you can begin the transformation to healing and wholeness.

• Start from a position of love. When God was planning what to do with His relationship to us, He was already loved. Within the Trinity, God is in an eternal love relationship. John 17:24 reminds us that the Father had always loved Jesus, even before the foundation of the world. God did not need us, and that is an important principle to remember as we establish and work out our relationships. If we need any one person in order to survive, we will not be able to resolve or build a healthy relationship. When we are dependent, we are not able to be ourselves and do the right thing. We become enablers and compromise ourselves to have our basic needs met.

LOVING OTHERS ACTION POINTS

Put these relationship principles into action now:

• Find people who value you and build from mutual love and respect. Don't try to force-feed somebody who's not hungry for the gift that God placed in you. If they can't see your value, they are not meant for you.

• Go where you're celebrated, not where you're tolerated. Learn from Leah (Genesis 29:31-35). She kept trying to win Jacob's love and affection using God's blessings (children). But she used the blessings for the wrong reason.

• Recognize toxic relationships and know when to walk away. A bad relationship creates constant unhealthy disagreement and strife (Amos 3:3). A toxic relationship hides you and holds you to your past. Watch out for predators of the heart. And if you are in a toxic relationship, walk away!
Practical steps to "love"

Love God. Love Yourself. Love Others.

REFLECTIONS

Write a summary of what "God's Love" means to you in your words.

_____
_____
_____

_____
_____
_____
_____

What does the Word of God say about love?

_____
_____
_____
_____
_____
_____
_____

Do a bible study on love. Write out how you can apply what you find in your life.

_____
_____
_____
_____
_____

Think of a time when someone showed you love through their actions.

_____
_____
_____
_____
_____
_____
_____

Write the name of one of the people you love in your life. Then write five ways you can show him or her God's love.

_____
_____
_____

What were the three important acts of love from the chapter?

_____

_____

_____

_____

_____

_____

_____

What can you do to fulfill those areas? Write a plan of action.

_____

_____

_____

_____

_____

_____

What does "Living In Love" mean to you?

_____

_____

_____

_____

_____

_____

What can you do to help others understand LOVE?

_____

_____

_____

_____

_____

_____

EXPERIENCE GOD'S PROVISION AND DIVINE PURPOSE!

Check out these other inspiring books
from Paula White:

First Things First
You're All That!
52-Week Success Planner
Fasting Made Simple
Daily Treasures
Deal With It!
He Loves Me
I Don't Get Wholeness... That's the Problem
Move On, Move Up
Principles for Processing Your Promise
Restoration-The Power of the Blood
A Sensational Life!

Also, go online to www.paulawhite.org for other inspiring resources
including articles, CD & DVD series, downloadable products,
partnership information, and so much more!

NOTES